How to Stop Living Paycheck to Paycheck:

How to take control of your money and your financial freedom starting today

Volume 1

By

Income Mastery

copy of the work or a recorded copy and is only permitted with the express written consent of the author. All additional rights reserved.

The information on the following pages is generally considered to be a truthful and an accurate description of the facts and, as such, any lack of attention, use or misuse of the information in question by the reader will cause the resulting actions to be solely within his or her competence. There are no scenarios in which the publisher or author of this book can be held responsible for any difficulties or damages that may occur to them after making the information presented here.

In addition, the information on the following pages is intended to be for informational purposes only and should therefore be regarded as universal. As befits its nature, it is presented without warranty with respect to its prolonged validity or provisional quality. The trademarks mentioned are made without written consent and can in no way be considered as sponsorship of the same.

Table of Contents

Introduction

How do you take control of your money and your time? How can you enjoy your money and be able to save it at the same time? How can you achieve financial freedom and be the boss of your life? We'll explain different ways to achieve financial freedom and take control of your money and your time today.

Let's start by thinking about what financial freedom is for you. To be able to travel whenever you want? To be able to give up office work from nine to five. To have no debt. To live off your interest. To be able to retire at fifty without worries. We all have different answers but financial freedom can be achieved in the same way. It is very important to take control of our finances and to avoid living worried and stressed, paying debts and working overtime in order to pay our bills. We have to start with a clear idea of what we want to do and why we want this freedom, this will give us a direction and will give us a clearer idea of our budget.

Achieving financial freedom can be achieved in a number of ways, not necessarily by making more money. We should start by getting our finances in order and to saving money. Is it possible to save your money and enjoy it at the same time? The answer is yes.

Knowing how to save and spend our money is critical to achieve financial freedom. Saving is not easy, spending is. It may seem impossible especially if you have never had control of your finances. This includes managing your credit cards, paying your debts, creating short- and long-term budgets, managing your monthly expenses, short- and long-term goals, amongst others. All this planning can intimidate us if we haven't done it before, but it's a matter of organization and a little work. Saving money and achieving financial freedom is learning to make conscious decisions, having determination, motivation and flexibility. We're not going to tell you that it's easy to take control of your money, but it's possible and every step of the way is worth it. Once you begin this process, you will realize that you are more disciplined than you think and that you will be able to achieve your goals without putting as much effort as you thought.

We will develop topics related to our management with credit cards, we will explain about the different types of expenses and how to eliminate or minimize them, We will also teach you how to create a budget in the short and long term, what it consists of, how they differentiate and we will teach you how to set goals you can achieve and how to achieve them. We will also explain how to organize your debts, what are the options to have lower interest rate. We will continue to use your credit, debit and cash cards. What is the difference between using them and why does it affect your savings? What is the impact of using both on your finances and how does it affect your personal freedom? This will impact and directly affects our savings and financial freedom.

In this volume we will teach you how to achieve financial freedom with simple but effective strategies.

Chapter I: How to prepare a real budget?

Let's start this process. The first thing we need to do before we start working on our budget is to evaluate our financial health. It is very important to know how much debt we are in; we need to know which Banks we owe money to, we also need to understand what is the interest rate that each debt has and what is the total amount that we need to pay. Once we have the full amount of our debts, we need to evaluate if we can pay them in one instalment or how long it will take us to pay them fully. This gives us an indication of how we are financially and what measures we should take. We must pay our debts in order to save most of our money.

Once we have calculated our debts, we can begin to assemble our budget which will include our income and expenses. It is very important to be honest with ourselves and add all the debts we have no matter how small. Once this is done, we have to analyze what kind of debts we have. Do they accrue interest? Is it possible to pass all our debts to a single entity? Realistically, how soon can we pay for them without putting the rope around our necks? It is very important to know how much the interest rate on our cards is and how it is calculated. Banks offer to purchase debt and place it in monthly fees with a fixed interest rate usually lower than the interest rate on our credit card. If you want to pay your debts in fixed fees and your bank offers this option at a good interest rate, you should consider the amount you must pay monthly and the amount of fixed fees which your bank allows you to accommodate them. The more you pay upfront, the less we have to pay each month. There are banks that allow us to pay our debts and fees monthly up to 3 years.

Everything will depend on the plans we have and how much we are willing to save in order to pay our debts faster which is what we recommend. Bear in mind in mind that we can also make payments to the capital of the debt without paying interest. Paying our debt in this way will help us enter the credit financial system and qualify for credit. It is very important that we pay our debts on time. This will give us a good credit score. We can also consider for another bank to buy our debt. For example, if you have debts with Bank A, Bank B will probably be able to buy the total amount with a smaller percentage of what Bank A offers. In this case, we could move the debt and put it into installments as well.

Once we have analyzed which is the best option for us, we can begin to elaborate our budget. It's easier to start with a short-term Budget which one from one to three years, and then continue to work on our long-term Budget which is from four to ten years.

Let's start by asking how much is our income? We must take into account not only our monthly income but whether we will have any additional income or not the additional income to take into consideration can be interest from our savings account, a birthday gift in cash that we receive every year, or perhaps income from renting property. We must take into account real numbers, do not add that increase that might come or some freelance work that could get offered to us. It is necessary that these numbers are realistic and true and that we take into account the amount of taxes to be paid. Once we have this number, we'll continue with the expenses.

We will start with the fundamental expenses such as the rent of our apartment or house or our mortgage, food and drinks you consume, monthly utilities (water, electricity, electricity, water, etc.), our transportation expenses and the amount we pay for our insurance. All of these expenses are essential and most are fixed. Utilities can vary from month to month depending on usage, so it's important to use the month with the most expenses and use it in our budget as our fixed monthly expense to save surprises. If the expenses are less than expected, it is important to keep that amount saved that month and use it to pay our debts that would be more convenient.

We also have to consider our intermittent expenses which will vary throughout the year such as the maintenance of our car or taxes that we must pay as vehicle tax each quarter. We should also consider if it is cheaper to pay annually s such as health insurance. Many companies offer discounts to their customers if a payment is made for a longer period of time. This alternative should be considered in order to try to minimize and reduce our expenses as much as we can.

One way to a budget is to take into account all the expenses we have made in the previous twelve months, analyze them and divide them by twelve. This will give us an idea of how much we have spent the previous month and year, what we have spent on and how our spending fluctuates. Seeing how much we've spent is also going to help us reconsider our spending. When we realize how much we spend on coffee daily, it will be easier for us to reconsider our habits and become more aware of the purchases we make. We recommend increasing this amount by ten or fifteen percent because it will help us to have an emergency fund for any additional unbudgeted payment such as a car repair or an emergency repair needed in our house or apartment. It also helps us in case of any unexpected increase in any of our accounts. If we do not use this amount, instead of spending it on items that we do not need and we can consider luxury. Little by little, with a little discipline, we will begin to save more money and will be able to achieve financial freedom.

For our short-term budget, it is very important to take into account the fixed membership fees of our credit cards, many people do not take into account this amount although it is a considerable amount if we have more than one card. This amount will vary depending on the financial institution and the type of card we have. We should start by checking how many credit cards we have and which ones we usually use. In the case of having more than one card from the same bank which is usually the case, we recommend verifying what is the interest rate of purchases per card and consult if you can unify lines, this way, we can save the membership payment. Unifying them mean s an increase on our credit line in case of an emergency.

It is also important to know how much is the minimum monthly expense that we must generate in order not to pay for this membership. What requirements does the bank have to be exonerated from it? It is very important to evaluate it since if we have too many credit cards that do not generate benefits it is better to evaluate if it is better to cancel it. Is it really worth paying for four or five different memberships annually? Do we use all the cards? These questions will help us plan which is going to be the best strategy for managing our money and credit cards, which ones we cancel and which ones we keep.

How to make this decision? We have to ask ourselves what is the benefit that we have with each card, we have to revise what is the interest rate applied in our purchases if we cannot pay with cash or if we cannot pay the total amount of money spend to the bank. We also need to take into consideration, if the card allows us to pay in installments without interests, if it offers us some added value like discounts in purchases in stores where we buy regularly. This simple exercise will help us save money. It will reduce our expenses and help us achieve of our short- and long-term goals. It will also change the relationship we have with credit cards, once we realize what is the additional item, we must pay for an item by paying it with credit card instead of paying it in cash, we will think about using it twice.

Now that we have our budget (we have subtracted our expenses from our actual income) and have made important decisions about our credit cards, we must ask ourselves if we have any money left, if we have a deficit or a surplus. We need to be certain that we can save money and if we have a deficit, we need to make sure we cut expenses.

Savings are achieved when our expenses are less than our income which allows us to save money, no matter how small. We also recommend saving for an emergency fund. This can be used in case of an emergency; we can also use this to our debts and this extra amount saved can also help us to generate more interest in our savings account which means we can obtain more income. It should not be seen as money that can be used in any situation, as the name implies, it is only for emergencies such as some treatment at the hospital related to our health. Doing this simple calculation will help us on our way to financial freedom, since we will know how much we spend monthly. This number will determine how much we can save or how much or many expenses we have to cut or reduce and which ones. We should always consider that it is possible to increase our income in different ways, not necessarily with a salary increase in our job but we can also have an additional job such as working for FreeLancer, we can, invest or switching to a type of savings account that generates more interest. This must be assessed by analyzing different Banks, their pros and cons, our time and what we really want.

Chapter II: Reducing Your Expenses

Speaking of savings, at this point, we can't help but look at our expenses. Why? Knowing what we spend on, how much we spend, how we spend and what our priorities are is going to help us on the road to financial freedom.

The most obvious answer to saving and reducing our expenses is that we have to start living below our income It sounds like an obvious answer, but it's not. We have to ask ourselves why to do we overspend? Why do we get into debt using our credit cards and paying very high interest rates? Do we really need to spend money on items which are not necessary for us_? Are these items vital to our happiness? Can we live without these expenses?

Let's start with expenses that we can cut and/or reduce and analyze our subscriptions. How many subscriptions do we have with automatic debit or debit to the credit or debit card? Are all our subscriptions really necessary?

Can we find an alternative? Is it really necessary to have Spotify Premium? Is Netflix vital to our life? Are we really using that gym membership? Do we have to go to the most expensive gym?

The first month we recommend at least cutting off one subscription and the following week or the following month another one. , We recommend looking for alternatives to see where we can watch movies or series on the Internet, where we can listen to music, if we can download it in another way or what would be the cheapest alternative. This will validate our decision and make us feel that we are not losing part of our comfort. You will realize that you do not need to make these expenses and that that money is better invested in the payment of your debt or that it can be saved in order to achieve that financial freedom you want so much. Do you have to work so many hours a day to be able to pay those subscriptions? The answer is really no.

As we have already mentioned, it is really important to start making conscious decisions and to be disciplined. When we begin to see the amount of money, we have saved, we will feel more motivated. Before buying something new, it is very important to ask ourselves what the purpose of the purchase is we are going to make. Will that new pair of shoes or wallet help us obtain the increase we want? Will it help us obtain the financial freedom? Where will it be better invested? These items will not help us gain financial freedom and will be better invested in a savings account earning interest. This type of non-vital expenses can be cut and that surplus can be used to pay off our debts or can be saved. Does it really make a difference to cut and/or reduce these expenses? Of course, adding them together, we realize that if we spend fifty dollars a month, we spend annually six hundred dollars that can be invested, in four years it will be two thousand four hundred dollars that could be used to pay the capital of our debts or saved. How long have we had these subscriptions? Let us remember that the more we save in less time, the faster we will achieve financial freedom.

We must take into account the costs of our house if we rent it. We have to analyze the price of it. Let's ask ourselves if the price is within the market, if we could live somewhere nearby with similar features for a cheaper price, if it's really worth spending so much money on this particular rental. Why would you prefer to live in a more expensive place if you could save hundreds of dollars a year for a place with the same features nearby or even on the same block? This change of mentality and the possibility of moving to a new house is going to mean big savings. Having a lower rent will mean that we can use that extra money to pay off our debts or save it so we can pay a higher down payment on a house and not have such a high interest debt. Most financial experts recommend not accepting any deal that costs more than one-third of your income. This is something we must consider, if we get a hundred dollars cheaper monthly housing per year are one thousand two hundred dollars saved that will help us get financial freedom, we will have control of our time and money.

On the other hand, we have to reconsider our costly expenses related to our habits. Do you smoke cigarettes? Do you drink a lot of alcohol? Do you do drugs? These habits can turn into costly addictions that can turn into serious health problems that would only lead us to continue spending our money. By quitting smoking you will see the difference not only in your savings but also in your body and health. We also recommend cutting back on the number of times you go out to drink alcohol per week with friends and don't use drugs. This will generate huge savings and you'll be one step closer to financial freedom.

Chapter III: Learn how to research, evaluate expenses and tips to save more money

One key to saving is to start researching everything we buy, analyzing and comparing prices. Many times, for our own convenience we go to the same supermarket or order the things we want online without doing much research and without much planning. How many times have we gone to the supermarket without a list of ingredients or what we should buy? This only generates additional purchases of what we think we are going to consume or what we feel like   at that moment. Without a list, we end up buying additional things because we don't know what we're going to cook and often end up throwing food away. Above all, how many times have you been into the supermarket feeling hungry and you end up buying items you   that you will never consume and that end up in the garbage can? Meal planning is critical to saving. When doing so, don't forget to take into account prices and expiration dates. Keep in mind that consuming any type of meat daily is going to be more expensive than consuming it four times a week and the remaining three days consuming beans and legumes. You can do easy exchanges such as   buying the cheaper cut of meat cut of meat and you can look for cheaper protein alternatives. Not only will it be healthier for you, but it will also help you save money

We have to take into account the expiration date of the items we are buying, usually we do not review them and we are surprised that the following week has already expired. This will prevent us from throwing away items like ham, cheese, cookies, yogurt or items we usually forget we have in the refrigerator and pantry. When shopping at the supermarket, don't forget to compare prices and pay attention to the weight and price difference between brands. Many times, the brand of the same supermarket is cheaper, but that is not always the case. Let's look for brands that we trust but are cheaper. Those ten-cents do make a difference in our savings.

Coupons and discounts offered by supermarkets and those that we can find on the Internet help us save even more money. Coupons are a great way to save money when shopping in supermarkets. Most supermarkets have a loyalty program or have coupons or special offers. Find out what the discounts are in the supermarket you go to, if there are special discounts depending on the day or where you can get coupons. Some supermarkets have electronic machines that print them. We always recommend entering or following the supermarket page in social networks as they are usually posting different promotions. These small savings make a big difference monthly and annually. We also recommend comparing local supermarket prices with the wholesale supermarket and with other supermarkets or places where we can buy our groceries.

It might seem tedious to have to be comparing and looking for different places to do our shopping, but most supermarkets have prices and catalogs on the web, even some supermarkets are cheaper if we order our groceries online via delivery than going to buy local. Remember we also need to add the cost of transport. If we decide to buy in a wholesale market that usually has better prices and offers, we must find where to store a greater number of products in our home. Although it may seem difficult at first, buying wholesale is often beneficial because not only do we save on food, but we also spend less on transport. Instead of going shopping on a weekly basis, we can make our monthly purchases. This will also help us plan more for our meals and our monthly budget. After a few months, we will adjust to this new planning and even find more ways to save at the supermarket.

Another tip for your shopping is to use a basket and not a car, especially if you're shopping on time. Using the cart is more comfortable, but we tend to buy more because we see them empty and we do not have to load it, it has no weight. When we use the basket as we have to carry it, we tend to want fewer things and less weight therefore it is more uncomfortable.

You should also be careful not to go to the supermarket during rush hour. Many times, we see the other person's cart and we see some product that we had not seen or wanted to buy so you buy it. We can avoid this by going to hours where there aren't as many people, going in focus and with our weekly, two-week or monthly shopping list. It's also better to go alone. If we go with family or friends, we tend to buy more. Usually because we don't pay attention, talk and the other person tends to give us recommendations and new ideas or dish suggestions for cooking, this increases our food budget unnecessarily.

With these tips we can maximize our savings on our supermarket purchases and our food. We must be disciplined so as not to fall into temptation or laziness to cook. Some tips are to cut all the vegetables in one day as soon as we buy them so that everything is ready and not having to be doing it every time we want to cook.

On a daily basis, we recommend paying attention to the small expenses we make without even realizing how much it affects our pocketbook and budget. The coffee we drink daily, that lunch sandwich, or the daily dessert we eat every day or every week means more expenses and less savings. Even that daily bottle of water or soda adds to our expenses. Sound familiar? Is this something you do? The question is, how can we generate more savings when we are away from home? If you're working in an office, can we bring our own food to work instead of going out to different restaurants for lunch every day? In case we can't take our food to work and we have to go out to eat we have to analyze which restaurant we have nearby. Are you hungry at eleven o'clock in the morning and do you eat sandwich? Bring a fruit from home or prepare something and anticipate this expense. Not only will your health improve, but you'll also start saving, and you'll have that money for yourself.

In case you have to go out for lunch, you need to do some research. Many restaurants have an executive menu that is cheaper than a la carte ordering. Many websites offer reservations at different restaurants with discounts of up to fifty percent if you book by that means. With these tips the lunch budget can be greatly reduced. These lunches must be properly budgeted for this reason it is so important to conduct prior research and anticipate these expenses. Ask yourself if we should really go out and eat in restaurants more than once or twice a week being able to cook at home and having the supplies to do so. How much do you spend on food? How much are you really spending on these sandwiches or these street food cravings? When we do the cost-benefit analysis we realize that by cutting these expenses and budgeting for outings to restaurants or cafes, we can save annually and/or pay our debts in less time. Are you going out with friends or family? Find and suggest a place where you don't have to consume so much, have a discount or have found a coupon.

Can you plan where to meet? Go to your friends' house, share the cost of food with everyone, or get together, but eat before you go out. This way, you'll avoid the temptation to order that pizza or hamburger when you're hungry. The most important thing in this case is to stick to it and respect the budget created. Are you going out to a bar with friends or colleagues? Have dinner at your home before so you don't have to order food during or after your departure. Ask for Happy Hour or After Office promotions or the drink of the day. You can share that two for one with one of your colleagues, moderate the amount of drink you order on your outings in order to achieve your financial freedom. These little tips help us generate and increase our savings and take us one step closer to financial freedom. It seems simple, but it requires motivation, willpower and determination. It's just a matter of planning and analysis.

Do you know how much you spend on transportation to and from work, home to friends or family, weekend outings, and shopping? When it comes to transport and savings, it is very important to know how much we are spending and what distances we are travelling. Can we see options such as taking public transport or the only way to get to our destination is driving? How close do we live? Can we generate any savings if we take a taxi or if we use a bicycle? Do you live close to people who work with you or go to the same destination and could they share a car or a taxi? These factors must be analyzed since it can allow us to reduce our expenses. In case we drive, using the car not only generates stress but also increases the mileage to your car reducing its value, increases your expenses in gasoline and in maintenance and repairs.

Begin by investigating what the public transport alternatives are, the prices and the route.

Can you walk or use the bicycle? Start by changing little by little, make a change and use the chosen means of transport twice a week, then three and in a short time you will get used to it. You'll have enough confidence that you'll always be able to mobilize yourself in this way to work, your social gatherings or wherever you need to go. You probably like it more than driving and you're more relaxed. The best option will always be to walk or ride a bicycle because apart from the fact that it has no cost, it has the plus that does not pollute, you can do your daily exercise, improve your health, reduce your stress and reduce your carbon footprint. Imagine how much you can save if you stop spending that hundred dollars a week, that's four hundred dollars a month and four thousand eight hundred soles a year. Did you already know how much you spend on transportation? Are you surprised?

Chapter IV: Learn to manage your credit cards

Do you understand how credit cards work_? To save we must understand how credit cards work, we must use them cautiously or only in emergencies if absolutely necessary. Do you know how much interest you have on the credit card? Do you know how it is calculated? Cards are very good for entering the banking system and applying for credit for buying a house or a car, but is it really necessary to use them when we go out or buy different items? The answer is no. We don't recommend taking your credit cards on outings with friends, when you go to the supermarket or when you go shopping with someone. The problem is, when we go out, we get excited and overspend. One more drink can't be that expensive, that polo shirt looks great on me or that pair of shoes will look great on me. For this reason, we recommend carrying cash for what we are going to use.

Cash must be within our budget and we recommend taking it exactly to buy or pay what we need punctually.

When paying in cash at an establishment, we recommend keeping the change in a small bag and not spending it. This will increase as the months go by and we will have an additional fund without much effort. Banks have machines that change the simple into bills, this additional money should be credited to the account that generates interest or your savings account. Don't spend it and put it away. You'll notice how easily you spend without realizing it in a month and especially in a year.

If we have not withdrawn the cash, we recommend paying with the debit card because it is cash and does not generate a debt, not with the credit card. The day we go out to eat or want to buy something, it is better to check beforehand with which stores and companies our bank has a discount because they have several alliances with different stores. This allows us to buy that item we need but spend less.

On the other hand, if we have been using the credit card regularly, it is also good to review what kind of agreements it has and if our expenses have generated something positive, have we been accumulating points? What kind of points? How many points do we have and how and on what can we redeem them? Most credit cards have agreements with airlines and we can exchange our points for airline tickets.

In our short- or long-term budget will we have to make a trip? If the answer is yes, we may redeem these accrued miles instead of making the fare payment or paying less fare. It is important to travel in low season and not in high season so that tickets, establishments and food have a lower cost and reduce our budget. Points awarded by banks can usually not only be redeemed for miles, many times they are also used for hotel nights, shopping in supermarkets and even in different stores of clothing or items. This way, we can save on our next purchase.

To save it is necessary to plan the trips in advance, we recommend planning them at least one year in advance to have better prices on air tickets, hotels and tours if we need them. Also, for tours we can always find free tours for tourists. Planning always helps us save money.

Do you have applications on your cell phone that have your credit card number and information? We usually have our credit cards in food applications for our phone's delivery of items or taxis. We recommend removing the information from the card and switching to the cash payment option. It's easier to fall into temptation if we don't have cash and want to ask for something and the laziness wins. We lose the account and begin to accumulate debts because consumption is not always charged at the time of consumption. Changing all your payments to cash will make you think twice before placing an order and will make you respect your budget. It's also easier to track your spending if all payments are in cash. The next time we want to order food form the application we will think twice if that amount is out of our monthly budget and we will have to sacrifice something for that order. Thus, we will begin to cook and make better, more conscious decisions and think about what we are spending. Welcome to the world of savings and planned decisions.

What are you using technology for? Are you using it the best way? We recommend using technology as your ally. How? Automate all your monthly payments to be made directly from your savings account. This way, you'll save yourself the stress of having to pay online or going to different locations to make different card payments. It is also a very good tool and a way to be cautious and not pay more than the bill in interest. For example, if we go on a trip and/or forget to pay for a card, financial institutions generate and charge high interest per day that the debt has not been repaid. This expenditure, is absolutely unnecessary. For this reason, by automating our payments we can save ourselves this additional stress. We can pay our utilities in this way also we only have to affiliate our account to these entities and generate a direct collection. Of course, we have to check that we're not being overcharged.

A useful tool to save is to open a savings goals account in our bank, this can be done from the application, there is no longer a need to go to the bank and make those long queues and lose half a morning. This type of account parallels our savings account and helps us reach the goal we consider attainable in the time we determine. How does it work and why does it help us save? Because we cannot withdraw that money when we please or want to buy something that is not in our budget, we must continue to contribute and keep that money until we reach the goal set and agreed with the bank. The only way to withdraw the money is to close the account. This money would still go back into our savings account, but the idea is to keep it where we can't be tempted to use it. This is very useful for us since we can fix the monthly amount that we can contribute and is according to our budget to this account and also request the automatic debit from our savings account, in this way, we cannot have this cash that helps us save and reach the amount we have set as a goal.

We recommend logging in sporadically to see the amount we have already saved on our accounts with relatively little effort. This will help us to motivate ourselves and continue to create the habit of saving. We will also be surprised how some changes and adjustments in our habits can generate significant savings. It is important, and this is what we recommend, to have the application of our bank in the cell phone in order to periodically review the expenses we have made and what is the total amount of our debts. Seeing how our savings are decreasing and how they are increasing, motivates us to continue saving. Financial freedom is getting closer and closer.

On the other hand, continuing with technology, there are several very easy to use applications that help you to keep your expenses up to date. In these applications we can add our monthly, daily and even annual budget and add our daily expenses. It will automatically tell us how much we have left to spend daily and what our income is after these expenses. Seeing our expenses and adding them to the application will also help us make more conscious decisions and give us a clearer idea of what expenses we could still adjust or even eliminate.

Some of these applications can be linked to our bank account and even include coupons and offers to help us save a little more. Without effort and without thinking it we will be reducing, even more, our expenses therefore we will be increasing our savings.

Chapter V: Learn to Save

Are you having trouble saving alone? Saving is also like exercising, if you do it with some friends or family, you get more motivated and you feel compelled to do it, it can even increase your competitiveness and you want to win by saving. There are some applications where you can create a savings group by inviting your family and friends. Each account and goal are individual as is the contribution, but it is very good for achieving goals together and motivating each other. Would you be interested in making a bet with your friends or family that you can save more? Download this type of application and start saving today. It should be noted that we must verify that these applications do not have commissions, have a minimum balance or any type of commission per transaction which is the case in the vast majority. It is very important to be motivated and know that saving is a matter of planning and making conscious decisions. Your friends and families can help you reach your goals and not buy too much.

Do you love shopping online? Do you always get the offers of your favorite brands? Do you get discounts from more than twenty different stores? This is the case for most people. How to stop falling into temptation of getting items which are on sale? If you are registered to receive promotions on your email of several stores it is time to unsubscribe or send all these emails to SPAM. This will prevent us from falling into the temptation to buy what we don't need when it's at a discount. We need to start making rational, non-emotional purchases. You have to stop buying because we see an item that we liked at a discount that will end up saved because we don't need it and we can consider it a luxury item. Don't window shop. that you can't buy! You'll want to include them in your budget or just to get them. Not being on the list of senders of this type of mails also removes the stress of wanting to buy something that is not planned or that we have not thought we need.

Some new item like a blender when ours still works perfectly, but the one we want has additional features we'll never use, but we think we need it. Sounds familiar? If we want to sign up and send us emails, we recommend that they are about finances, how to achieve your goals and financial tips. This will keep us motivated and educate us more in the management of our finances. Subscribe to pages you like; do you practice any sport? Are you interested in a particular topic? Start using your time in whatever you want and whatever you like.

These small tips prevent us from making small purchases that add up at the end of the month and help prevent us from falling into temptations.

Returning to the use of cards, in case you need to use the credit card and cannot pay the full amount before it generates interest, call your bank and ask them to put it in installments. Why do we do this? So, we don't pay interest and have to pay the bank more than the item alone cost us. Remember that the interest is calculated on the total amount we have not paid, that is, if your interest on purchases is fifty percent and you could not pay one hundred dollars, we will have to pay the additional half of the item purchased. Have you thought about it this way before? Imagine how much more we have paid to the banks for not paying the full amount of our debts.

This is going to be that we respect our budget for our departures and do not spend more than we should. We can also see how much we are actually spending. As we have recommended, it is very important to know how much we are spending, and to add all our expenses to some of the applications in the cell phone that we have chosen and that help us determine this amount. Knowing what we are spending on we can also cut additional costs, for example, if our daily food spending budget is twenty dollars, we can see what we are actually spending on. We'll think twice before we buy that coffee we can have at home.

Another way to save a little more without much effort is to search for coupons on the internet. There are websites that offer discounts in restaurants, hotels and restaurants. But the most important thing is to think before buying something we don't need.

To establish our short-term savings goal, we can start planning for one to three years. We should think about saving so that we can live from three to nine months to pay the daily expenses just in case, since we don't know what could happen in the future in the company where we work or in the economy of our country. We must save cash to pay for our vacations and large purchases like a car. The long-term savings plan should be four years or more and should include the startup of a home or remodeling project, the education of your children, and the retirement you so much dream of. We may also consider investing our money in an investment account which, while representing a risk, also indicates an opportunity to grow as the market grows.

Setting a smaller savings goal, such as buying a cell phone, can give us the psychological boost that makes the immediate sense of saving rewarding and a habit.

In the social sphere, do you check everything you pay? It's a very bad habit, but we don't usually check the bills we pay or verify what we sign or check the ballot. Unbelievable, isn't it? How many of us are guilty of this?

We recommend that, if you're going out with friends and they ask for the bill at a bar, for example, that you verify that they haven't loaded any of their drinks into your account so that you don't overpay. Do your friends or family want to split the bill and you've only consumed one dish? Avoid doing this, explain that you are in savings mode and that you will only pay for what you have consumed. This will most likely prevent your bill from being three times more expensive than your consumption. Do you tip in restaurants? Consider downloading an application that calculates how much tip to leave and add it to your expenses.

Do you think saving is going to be boring? Do you think your social life is going to suffer or are you already stressed and missing those outings to bars and restaurants every weekend or three times a week? Do you think you won't be able to have fun because you are saving and can't go out with friends? That's not true. You can change your leisure and recreational habits for new and more affordable ones. This will help you find the perfect balance between fun and responsibility - you'll be saving, having fun and exploring at the same time! Try it and be surprised, you could have more fun and have new friends exploring these options.

Free events in your city? Yes! Stay on top of your community's free events, follow them on social networks, search for groups on Facebook or various community pages where people comment and share these types of events. Does my city have free events? Yes, all cities have an itinerary of free recreational activities for all citizens. For example, some of the free activities they do are screenings of different movies in parks, free classes in different sports, dance or aerobics, art exhibits, and community events funded by donations. Visit them and change your routine. You'll get more involved with the community, meet new people, and explore these new kinds of fun activities you wouldn't have experienced had it not been for this life change.

Lowering our recreational costs will help us save and stay within our monthly budget and may even help us save more than we have budgeted. On the other hand, if you're used to playing video games or buying games online or for the Nintendo Switch you can make a change and look for free games or just change activity or add it to our new day, we recommend you start reading. Reading is a free activity that you can do without spending money. There are pages and applications that provide complete and free books. Does your city and district have a library? There are many second-hand stores that have very cheap books. Try it and you'll see your savings account increase.

Do you know your city? Have fun exploring with your friends, doing activities like walking, without having to spend a lot of money or even anything at all. There are different cultural activities such as free museum nights, free tours of your city center and a range of activities you can do for free.

Are you worried about financial freedom in twenty years? Consider opening a retirement account. It is really important that we have this account in plans so that we can achieve financial freedom in the long term. If we want to achieve financial freedom, we need to start thinking about retiring.

When do you want to retire? On this will depend the amount of money that we will have to keep in order to retire earlier. While everyone's situation is different, experts recommend contributing at least ten percent of your monthly income to your retirement account so you can maintain your current lifestyle without worry. Does that sound like a high number? When you begin to make the small changes in your habits already mentioned you will realize that this number is attainable and that you could even contribute a little more. Another option is to check with your employer about contributing to a retirement plan. Companies have agreements and alliances with different financial centers so these accounts allow automatic deposits for a specific amount of your monthly salary. Consider that the money that is deposited into this specific account will not be subject to the same rates as the rest of your salary. Simple, isn't it?

Chapter VI: How to generate more savings

Do you want to save even more money? Then it is absolutely necessary that you start to pay attention to the amount of electricity you consume daily in our home. Do you sleep with the television on? Do you leave the lights on? Do you turn that room lamp off before going out or does it stay on all night and all morning? It may seem harmless and that consumption is not much, but these small oversights increase our monthly electricity bill accordingly annually and affect our savings goal. Using the drying machine daily or more than once a week also consumes a lot of electricity. We must take into account the time it takes to dry clothes to be able to program when and how we are going to wash our clothes in order to reduce our electricity consumption. The thermal also consumes electricity, in order to reduce it, can be turned off daily or when we go away from home for several days or holidays. These small changes will not only help to increase your savings but you will also be helping the planet.

These small changes in our daily habits have a positive impact on our finances. We have different options and simple strategies to start saving and achieve our financial freedom. Recover your time and control your money by following our advice. The first step will be to evaluate our financial health, how much do we really owe to the banks? Do we owe some other kind of entity? You have to start by being completely honest with yourself. Then we must see how we can pay this debt monthly without accumulating so much interest, we can talk to our financial institution and request a debt purchase. This means that we will have the option of paying in installments for a certain period of time at a lower interest rate. This gives us the opportunity to better organize our budget and lower the interest expense on purchases we have already made.

Therefore, we could convert our total debt into a fixed monthly installment for a certain number of times according to our goal and within our payment possibilities. We may also ask another financial institution to buy our debt and compare which one has the best interest rate for us. The type of payment would be the same. Once we have the exact amount of our debt, we must calculate how much money we actually have in the month, after we have paid our fixed and basic expenses. This will give us an idea at the beginning of what changes we need to make in order to start saving and how many expenses we need to reduce or cut.

Starting with simple actions like budgeting our expenses, using saving vouchers, amongst other actions. You need to know your monthly income and become aware of how much we spend and on what. By being aware and conscious of our expenses we can get out of our debts, save and find financial freedom. These small actions throughout the months and the year will lead us to gain financial freedom and regain control over our finances and our time. Some simple actions we can perform are to keep track of what we have spent after making each purchase daily, storing the vouchers and/or recording it in the application we have chosen for the cell phone that will carry our finances. With this exercise, we will realize the type of expenses we are making and which we can cut or decrease. We'll think twice before we buy that sandwich, coffee or pair of shoes that aren't within our budget and we don't need.

CONCLUSION

Subscriptions to different programs and/or applications make our monthly and annual expenses higher, especially if we have a program or application that can replace it. This is true for example in subscriptions such as Netflix or having a Spotify Premium account. We know that we can still listen to music and watch series on other websites or applications for free and that they are not exclusive and are not the only ones. On the other hand, analyzing our fixed costs will be very helpful in evaluating the changes we can make. Is our apartment or house rent too expensive? Can we find another place with the same characteristics for less money? How much can we reduce our consumption of water and electricity? By taking shorter showers, leaving the lights and television off as well as reducing the number of times we use the clothes dryer each month, we can reduce our electricity and water bills. Turn off the water heater when you go on a trip and disconnect your electronic devices, you will be surprised by the difference in your electricity and water bill.

Going to the supermarket without a list and thinking about buying whatever you choose with your finger, with your list in mind, as you walk down the aisles? Keep a list of the food and beverages that you must buy so that you don't buy more than the bill and that in the end you have food left. By planning our week menu or even if we can of the month, we can considerably reduce our expenses. By analyzing and reviewing competitor's prices, we can also choose to buy in the cheapest place and with the best offers. Reviewing the offers, discounts and coupons offered by different supermarkets and stores will help us get a better idea of where to buy.

In addition, there are several applications that offer coupons and discounts in different supermarkets and stores. How much do you spend on transportation to and from the supermarket? Buy at a wholesaler, you could make your purchases up to once a month this will lower the cost of your food, help you plan better, spend less on transportation and help reduce the emission of carbon dioxide and thus global warming.

Log in and look for coupons and discounts, so you can start spending less. Make better decisions when planning your social and family events. Don't forget that you must also budget all outings with friends, family and colleagues. Do you want to stay within your budget? Look for restaurants with discounts on different websites, applications or check if you have any type of discount on our debit card due to the financial institution with which we are affiliated. Did you go out with friends? It is necessary to keep track of what we are consuming and pay attention to our accounts. How many times do we actually review what we are being charged and what we are paying in cash or what we are getting back in a box? It is extremely important to review our accounts, ballots and/or invoices, what we are paying and our return.

In case you are in a group and want to divide the bill if you are the person who has consumed less it would be good to explain that you are saving and that you will only pay what you have consumed. It is very important that your fast food or taxi applications do not have your credit card registered to avoid consumptions and think that you will pay them later. Let's not let laziness beat us. Pay and change the payment method in all your applications to cash. This will force us to think and be aware of what we are spending on.

We must emphasize that we must stop using our credit cards in order to save on our daily purchases. This is due to the fact that the interest generated by the card if the total amount is not paid is very high, we can even pay double what we have bought or our debt. It's easier to keep our budget and respect it if we have the right cash for our payments, if we start using the credit card we can easily get out of our budget and spend more than we can or need.

How do we get around the city daily? This also influences our budget and our savings goal. It's one of those expenses that we can reduce by researching the best way to get to work, family gatherings, the supermarket, or our friends' house. Are you going by car? Do you know what expenses are involved? When riding in our own vehicle we spend on gasoline, maintenance and pollute the environment. Apart from that, we increase the mileage of the car, which reduces its market value. What do you do? Do you have a colleague who also drives a car and wants to share the costs? Better yet, can you get to the office by public transport? It is very important to compare prices to see how much the monthly and annual savings would be. If we work close to the office we may consider walking or cycling. These would be the best options since they are free, help with daily stress, you will be exercising before and after the office and will not pollute or affect the ozone layer.

To save money we can also look for other types of organized community activities such as outdoor cinema in parks, historical walks in our city or outdoor activities. Get involved in your community, have new experiences and enjoy more by paying less and saving less. We recommend that you keep all the returns we have when paying in cash at any establishment. A good idea would be to put it in a piggy bank. Monthly or quarterly we can go to the bank to exchange often for notes and deposit it in our savings account.

Use technology to your advantage. Talk to your bank and request automatic debit in the payment of your bills this will avoid the stress of going to the financial institution to pay monthly and carelessness if we go on a trip. Every day that passes that we do not pay a debt this sum interest. Are you not very convinced of how you can use the technology in your favor? Open an account from your bank's application with a savings goal of money you cannot use and request that this money be debited directly from your account. You'll be surprised how much we spend that seems so little. Challenge your family and friends to save, download an application and create a group to invite them to save with you, each goal and each deposit will be individual, but they will motivate each other. Download the application that carries your expenses, check them periodically, think that expenses such as coffees and dinners can reduce. Motivate and check periodically what is the amount you are already saving, check that all payments with automatic debit have been made and relax. Send SPAM or request that you no longer get discounted emails from your favorite stores, do you really need that new pair of shoes? Do you need that new working blender that you'll never understand or use? Not really.

All of these suggested changes will not only change our routine, they will also change your mentality and your relationship and understanding of finances and money. It will help you save in an easier way than the one you expected, we will be able to reach our goals and achieve financial freedom, we will learn and regain control of our money and time. These small changes in our daily routine will help us reach our financial goals, pay our debts and have our emergency fund. We shouldn't be stressed about money; we should have better handling. We don't necessarily need that increase or additional work, we must learn to reduce and minimize the additional luxury expenses we have and we must learn to make rational, conscious, planned and unemotional decisions. Start today and change your life! Save today!